INSIDE THE WORLD OF SPORTS

INSIDE THE WORLD OF SPORTS

AUTO RACING

BASEBALL

BASKETBALL

EXTREME SPORTS

FOOTBALL

GOLF

GYMNASTICS

ICE HOCKEY

LACROSSE

SOCCER

TENNIS

TRACK & FIELD

WRESTLING

INSIDE THE WORLD OF SPORTS
BASEBALL

by Andrew Luke

MC MASON CREST

Mason Crest
450 Parkway Drive, Suite D
Broomall, Pennsylvania 19008
(866) MCP-BOOK (toll free)

Copyright © 2017 by Mason Crest, an imprint of National Highlights, Inc.

First printing
9 8 7 6 5 4 3 2 1

Names: Luke, Andrew.
Title: Baseball / Andrew Luke.
Description: Broomall, Pennsylvania : Mason Crest, [2017] | Series: Inside
 the world of sports | Includes bibliographic references, webography and index.
Identifiers: LCCN 2015046927 (print) | LCCN 2016015610 (ebook) | ISBN
 9781422234570 (Hardback) | ISBN 9781422234556 (Series) | ISBN
 9781422284193 (eBook)
Subjects: LCSH: Baseball--United States--History.
Classification: LCC GV867 .L85 2017 (print) | LCC GV867 (ebook) | DDC
 796.3570973--dc23
LC record available at https://lccn.loc.gov/2015046927

QR CODES AND LINKS TO THIRD-PARTY CONTENT

CONTENTS

KEY ICONS TO LOOK FOR:

Words to understand: These words with their easy-to-understand definitions will increase the reader's understanding of the text while building vocabulary skills.

Educational Videos: Readers can view videos by scanning our QR codes, providing them with additional educational content to supplement the text. Examples include news coverage, moments in history, speeches, iconic sports moments and much more!

Text-dependent questions: These questions send the reader back to the text for more careful attention to the evidence presented there.

Research projects: Readers are pointed toward areas of further inquiry connected to each chapter. Suggestions are provided for projects that encourage deeper research and analysis.

The Commissioner's Trophy has been awarded to the winner of the World Series at the end of each MLB season since 1967. There was no official trophy for the champion prior to this. The design features gold flags representing each team rising above a silver baseball. A new trophy is made every year as the winners keep permanent possession of the trophy after they receive it on the field.

CHAPTER 1

BASEBALL'S GREATEST MOMENTS

Baseball is America's national pastime. That has long been the identity of the longest-enduring American sport. In the last generation, however, the game has lost some of that identity. The most popular sport of the baby boomer generation has been surpassed by football in terms of TV ratings and national prominence. The well-regarded Harris Poll has shown every year since 1985 that baseball is less popular with Generation X and now less popular still with Millennials.

The demise of baseball, however, is not imminent. National ratings may be down, but unlike football, baseball's television strategy is regional, and in its local markets, baseball ratings are very strong. Baseball, though, is not really built for TV like football is. Baseball is meant to be experienced at the ballpark.

More than 70 million people attend Major League Baseball (MLB) games every season. The baseball stadium experience is unique in all of sports. Classic stadiums become shrines, bucket list destinations. People plan special trips to go to Wrigley Field and Fenway Park. Stadiums are classically and carefully designed to be unique, like Camden Yards in Baltimore and AT&T Park in San Francisco. Let's face it; there is a lot of down time at a baseball game. But when you have a panorama like the one that greets fans at Pittsburgh's PNC Park, fans hardly notice the lulls.

Coming out of the tunnel into the stands overlooking a freshly cut diamond on a warm summer day is a sensory experience the quality of which cannot be matched by other sports. Baseball smells like summer, and the crack of the bat and the thump of cowhide on leather provide a distinct and unique soundtrack.

With its 162-game season and daily game frequency, baseball becomes the background to American summers. It becomes part of our lives. On the radio or on TV, during the season, a game is playing almost everywhere you go.

Baseball's stories are also part of the fabric of America. Some of the most classic moments in American sports have occurred between the foul lines on the diamonds of the past and present.

Ruth Calls His Shot

Babe Ruth is undeniably one of the best hitters in baseball history and is arguably the best ever to play the game. His numbers speak for themselves. His legend grew immeasurably, however, during the 1932 World Series.

His New York Yankees faced the Chicago Cubs in game three, and Ruth came to the plate to hit in the fifth inning under a barrage of insults from Cubs fans in the stands at Wrigley Field. Down two strikes in the count, film of the moment shows Ruth pointing out to center field. What was the exact meaning of the gesture? It makes no difference now. Ruth hit the next pitch nearly 500 feet into the centerfield bleachers for his second home run of the game, and the legend that he had declared that intention has lived in baseball lore forever.

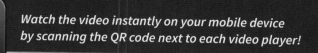
Gehrig's Farewell Speech

Ruth's teammate on the 1932 Yankees, Lou Gehrig, followed that famous at-bat by hitting a home run of his own. It was one of many in his brilliant career, a career that was cut tragically short by the illness that bears his name today. In 1939, Gehrig was diagnosed with amyotrophic lateral sclerosis. Lou Gehrig's disease is a fatal illness that attacks the nervous system.

Gehrig knew something was wrong during the 1938 season, which he finished with statistics well below his career averages. He played the first eight games of the 1939 season before going to the doctor. He retired mid-season on June 21, and the Yankees held Lou Gehrig Day on July 4, where they retired his number 4. During his speech at the ceremony, the terminally ill Gehrig referred to himself as "the luckiest man on the face of the Earth." There wasn't a dry eye in the house. Gehrig died in 1941. He was only 37.

Jackie Robinson Integrates Baseball

Gehrig's speech may be the most famous moment in baseball history, but the most important moment could well be the signing of Jackie Robinson in 1947. Robinson, an African American, was playing in the segregated Negro Leagues when Branch Rickey, president of the Brooklyn Dodgers, approached him. There were no black players in the Major Leagues, but Rickey wanted to change that. Rickey signed Robinson to a minor league contract in 1946, and then in 1947 Robinson was called up to the Dodgers before the season. He made his debut on April 15, 1947, breaking the race barrier and paving the way for other black players to be signed.

Despite being harassed and threatened by opposing teams and players, Robinson played well and was named Rookie of the Year for the season. By 1959, all teams had at least one black player. Every team in baseball has retired Robinson's number 42 as a tribute to his legacy.

The Shot Heard 'Round the World

Four seasons later, Robinson's Dodgers had a healthy lead late in the 1951 season. The 13 ½-game cushion over their National League rival New York Giants seemed insurmountable. The Giants, however, found their stride in the final 44 games, winning 37 of them to tie the Dodgers on the last day of the season.

A best-of-three playoff between the two teams came down to game three. In the first major sporting event ever to be televised nationally, things again looked bleak for the Giants. New York trailed 4–1 in the bottom of the ninth. The Giants managed to string together three hits to make the score 4–2 with two runners on base. Giants' outfielder Bobby Thomson strode to the plate to face relief pitcher Ralph Branca. Thomson watched the first two pitches before driving Branca's 1-1 offering into the left-field seats for the pennant-winning shot heard 'round the world.

Willie Mays' Catch

Dodger manager Chuck Dressen could have had Branca walk Thomson with first base open to set up a double play and a force out at every base. Next up for the Giants that day, however, was soon to be Rookie of the Year center fielder Willie Mays. Mays had a fearsome bat, but the most famous play of his career came courtesy of his glove.

In game one of the 1954 World Series, the Giants were tied 2–2 with Cleveland in the eighth inning. Cleveland had two runners on with Vic Wertz at the plate. Wertz belted a 2-1 pitch to deep center field. Mays quickly turned and ran full speed with his back to the plate. It looked like the ball would sail over his head, but he reached up and caught it in full stride without looking back. Mays saved the go-ahead run, and the Giants went on to win the game and sweep the series.

Watch the video instantly on your mobile device by scanning the QR code next to each video player!

Mazeroski's Home Run

Just as Mays was an offensive force who had a great moment with his glove (Mays was a true five-tool player), the opposite was true of West Virginia native Bill Mazeroski. Known as Maz, he was one of the best defensive second basemen of all time, winning eight Gold Gloves in his career with Pittsburgh. The Pirate's Hall of Famer forever will be remembered, however, for one mighty swing of his bat.

In the 1960 World Series, Pittsburgh and the Yankees were tied at three games each and nine runs each in the bottom of the ninth in game seven. Mazeroski was the first hitter of the inning, and he didn't bother to waste time building tension. Maz hit the second pitch over the left-field wall to end the World Series in dramatic fashion. It is the only game seven walk-off home run in World Series history.

April 8, 1974

Aaron Passes Ruth

One player who knew a thing or two about hitting home runs was Henry Aaron. "Hammering Hank" played 23 seasons, mostly with the Braves in Milwaukee, then Atlanta. Aaron hit at least 24 home runs for 17 straight seasons and hit more than 30 fifteen times, which is a record.

When Babe Ruth retired, he had 714 career home runs, one of the game's most hallowed records. In 1974, 21-time all-star Aaron started the season with 713. Media attention was unprecedented as the country awaited the inevitable fall of Ruth's 39-year-old mark. There was much negative attention as well, as racially motivated hate mail and death threats were commonplace for Aaron, a black man about to break a white hero's record. Aaron persevered, tying the record with his first swing of the 1974 season in Cincinnati then breaking it on April 8 in front of his home fans in Atlanta. He retired in 1976 with 755 homers.

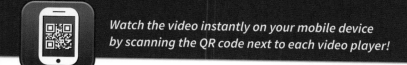
Fisk Waves It Fair

Ruth's record may have fallen in 1974, but in the mid-1970s, his curse was still going strong. The Boston Red Sox sold Ruth to the Yankees in 1919, and the Red Sox had not won a World Series since. In 1975, however, the Sox reached the World Series against Cincinnati but trailed the Reds three games to two as they played game six at Fenway Park in Boston.

The game stretched into extra innings tied 6-6. When Boston came to bat in the bottom of the 12th, the leadoff hitter was Carlton Fisk, their all-star catcher. Fisk hit the second pitch straight down the left-field line. One of the TV cameras showed Fisk as he wildly waved his arms to coax the ball to stay fair. It struck the pole above Fenway Park's famed Green Monster wall, and the Sox won game six. Of course, they lost game seven.

Gibson's Limp-Off Homer

Game one of the 1988 World Series started well for the Oakland A's as they scored four runs in the second inning and made that stand up until the ninth. The L.A. Dodgers were down to their final out, trailing 4-3. But closer Dennis Eckersley walked the next batter, allowing the winning run to come to the plate. That is when that year's National League most valuable player (MVP), Kirk Gibson hobbled out of the dugout to pinch hit. Injured in the National League Championship Series (NLCS), he had been taking practice swings in the clubhouse.

Gibson battled to a full count in obvious pain with every move. Then, in a scene right out of the movies, he hit a 3-2 pitch into the right-field stands. He limped around the bases, celebrating with a double fist pump. Announcer Vin Scully echoed the thoughts of millions when he said, "I don't believe what I just saw!" It was Gibson's only at-bat of the series, which L.A. went on to win.

Ripken Passes Gehrig

When Lou Gehrig tragically retired due to his terminal illness in 1939, it not only ended a brilliant career much too soon, but it also ended one of the most amazing streaks in the game's history. Gehrig had played 2,130 consecutive games. He played through fractures and concussions, always in the lineup for at least one at-bat. Gehrig was known as the Iron Horse for his unprecedented durability.

The record stood for 56 years, specifically until September 6, 1995, when it was broken by Baltimore Oriole third baseman Cal Ripken, Jr. The game in which he passed Gehrig is one of the most watched games in TV history–playoffs included. The president of the United States attended in person. No one knows how many games Gehrig might have played had he not become ill. Ripken went on to extend the streak to 2,632, when perfectly healthy, he decided to end the streak on his own terms.

Jeter Flips It Home

Another Hall of Famer, who ended things on his own terms, is New York Yankee shortstop Derek Jeter. Jeter retired in 2014, hitting a walk-off single to win his final game. In a career filled with accolades and World Series victories, however, there is one moment that stands out.

In the 2001 American League Division Series (ALDS), the Yankees faced Oakland. Trailing in the series 2-0, they had a 1-0 lead with two outs in the seventh inning of game three. Oakland's Jeremy Giambi was on first base and took off on a line drive into the right-field corner. With Giambi rounding third, the right fielder missed the cutoff men trying to throw home. But Jeter was sprinting to cover the first base line from his shortstop (SS) position and, in full stride, fielded the ball with his bare hand and shoveled it toward the plate. Giambi was tagged out, and the Yankees held on to win the game and the series.

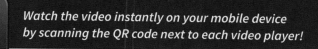

The Curse Is Broken

For 86 years, the Curse of the Bambino had persisted. In 1919, the Boston Red Sox famously sold Babe Ruth to the New York Yankees. Ruth, of course, blossomed into one of the best hitters of all time, leading the Yankees to many World Series victories. Boston, on the other hand, floundered. The Sox did come tantalizingly close, losing the series in seven games in 1946, 1967, 1975, and most memorably in 1986, when an extra-innings error by Red Sox first baseman Bill Buckner cost Boston game six.

The 2004 Red Sox, however, threw off the curse in dramatic fashion. They fell behind three games to none to the Yankees in the ALCS. But for the first time in baseball history, a team rallied to overcome a 3–0 series deficit as they defeated their archrivals in seven games. Boston then swept St. Louis in the World Series.

Honus Wagner 1911

 Words to Understand:

substantive: real or actual

cricket: a game, popular especially in England, with the object being to score runs by batting the ball far enough so that a player can exchange wickets with the batsman defending the opposite wicket before the ball is recovered

regiments: a military unit of soldiers on the ground, consisting of battle groups, a headquarters unit, and certain supporting units

CHAPTER

THE ORIGIN OF BASEBALL

You might hear a lot about a man named Abner Doubleday when people talk about the origin of baseball, but he did not invent the game. In fact, no one did. Baseball as the sport we know today evolved over centuries from a variety of different games. The first recorded description of a similar game comes from Greece around 1000 BC.

In 1908, Doubleday was credited with the game's invention in a report commissioned by National League president Abraham Mills. The report carried a lot of weight at the time. Baseball's Hall of Fame is based in Cooperstown, New York, because that is where the report said Doubleday invented the game. Many historians, however, have found the report to be untrue. The legend of Doubleday as inventor, however, still persists today, despite there being no evidence that he had any involvement with the game.

Fans watch an afternoon game at Wrigley Field on April 30, 2010, in Chicago, Illinois.

A COLONIAL SPORT

In America, versions of the game came across the Atlantic with 18th-century immigrants. From cat ball to town ball, there were different rules and methods, some involving bases, some without. The bat and the ball were the only constants. There was certainly no equipment like the gloves or catcher's mask that we associate with the game today.

In 1845 in New York City, a gentlemen's club member named Alexander Cartwright organized a team to play his version of the game. Named after the club, the Knickerbockers decided to formalize the game by actually writing down the rules. They established where on the field would be fair or foul territory and how much distance there would be between bases. That distance was set at the very inexact measure of 30 paces. Ninety feet (27.4 m) was established 22 years later. The common practice of hitting runners with the ball to put them out was replaced with tagging them or throwing the ball to a baseman in advance of the runner's arrival.

LATE CENTURY EVOLUTION

Cartwright's changes were the basis for the modern game. Baseball continued to evolve over the next 45 years. A base on balls requiring nine balls was gradually reduced to the four balls (and three strikes) we know today. For years, pitchers threw underhand from 45 feet (13.7 m) (later 50 [15.2m]) to a location requested by the batter. Overhand pitching came along in 1884. With overhand pitching came the need for self-preservation, so catcher's masks and chest protectors were invented. Catcher's mitts were not as quick to come into use, as those who did try to use hand protection took a great deal of ribbing from their barehanded compatriots.

The pitching rubber arrived in 1893, set 60 feet 6 inches (18.4 m) from home plate, which was still a 12-inches (30-cm) square. The plate became its present 5-sided 17-inches (43 cm) version in 1900. As far as **substantive** rule changes to the way the game is played goes, there have not been any since that time. Baseball, as to the rules the players follow, is so unchanged that players from 50, 100, or 120 years ago could appear at a stadium today, recognize the layout, and step up to the plate without a glance at the rule book.

THE BASEBALL TREND

Baseball quickly gained popularity over **cricket**, the most commonly contested and followed sport of the time. It had a much faster pace, taking just a few hours to complete versus several days for a cricket match. Other gentlemen's clubs began to pick up the game, beginning in Brooklyn, but also spreading up to Boston and all the way south to New Orleans. The game spread beyond social clubs to colleges and even businesses. It was liveries versus blacksmiths and carpenters against draymen doing battle on the diamond after a long week of work. Games between New York and Brooklyn during an Independence Day celebration would draw more than 10,000 spectators.

The game caught the eye of *New York Times* writer Henry Chadwick in 1856. Chadwick liked it so much, in fact, that when he moved to writing for the *New York Clipper* the next year, he convinced his editors that he should report on the games, which they allowed. Soon other writers followed suit, and the publicity made the game even more popular. Chadwick also implemented the first scoring system and box scores to track player results within games. These contributions have earned Chadwick recognition as the Father of Baseball.

THE PASTIME SPREADS

The first organized league formed in 1858. Twenty-five clubs dubbed themselves the National Association of Baseball Players (NABP) and played games against each other. By 1860, the association had 70 teams. The teams had flannel uniforms and straw hats and traveled hundreds of miles to play each other, with home teams graciously hosting visiting teams. There was friendly wagering, enthusiastic crowds, and newspaper coverage, making baseball games the social events of summer days.

1888 Philadelphia Quakers

During the Civil War from 1862 to 1865, the game was played in army camps and even between enemy **regiments** before battles. Soldiers from small towns or farms who had never seen the game took it back home with them after the war. This helped the NABP swell in membership from 70 teams before the war to 237 by 1867.

PROS AND PROFIT

The scourge of professionalism had been avoided in baseball to this point. There were suspicions, of course. Some thought hard-throwing pitcher Jimmy Creighton had been paid to pitch for Brooklyn in 1859. The first confirmed professional was Al Reach, a cricket player who took $25 a week to play for the Philadelphia Athletics in 1863.

As the game became more popular, rivalries grew between neighboring towns. There was pressure from civic leaders and residents alike to have a winning team for their community. This translated to managers who would hire players and investors who would fund the transactions. The demand for baseball had grown so much that so had the opportunity to turn a profit on it.

Text-Dependent Questions:

1. A controversial report commissioned by National League president Abraham Mills in 1908 credited whom with the invention of baseball?

2. For years, pitchers threw underhand from 45 feet (13.7 m) to a location requested by the batter. Overhand pitching came along in what year?

3. What did the first organized baseball league call itself after forming in 1858?

Research Project:

Take a look at the salaries earned in baseball over time, and compare them to those of other sports by creating a chart or graph to detail how each sport's salaries have changed over the years.

1869 Cincinnati Red Stockings

 Words to Understand:

disbanded: broken up or dissolved (as in an organization)

immigrants: people who migrate to another country, usually for permanent residence

persisted: continued firmly in some state, purpose, or course of action, especially in spite of opposition

CHAPTER

THE BIG LEAGUES ARE BORN

In Cincinnati, they were serious about their baseball. The community badly wanted a winning team, and in 1869, a group formed that was determined to achieve that goal.

THE FIRST PRO TEAM

This group of businessmen funded the hire of cricket star Harry Wright to manage the Cincinnati Red Stockings (named for their prominent footwear). Wright also was given a budget of $9,500 to go out and hire the best players, and that's exactly what he did, starting with his own brother.

The Red Stockings were a powerhouse, going 57-0-1 as they toured the nation pulverizing opponents. The 1869 Cincinnati team stayed together only for that one season, but around the country, other people of means got the idea, and professional baseball was born. The early years, however, were far from stable.

THE FIRST PRO LEAGUE

In Chicago, an owner named William Hulbert started a league of professional teams called the National League in 1876, which included the Red Stockings. His league had a collection of rules designed to make the National League a stable entity, including no Sunday games and no beer sales in the stands. Gambling was an issue, however, among both the fans and the players. Many fans also preferred to continue watching their town teams rather than these newly formed pro teams. Teams lost money and **disbanded**.

Players tried to start their own nine-team league, but this was short-lived as players had no contracts, jumping from team to team, with some teams choosing which scheduled games they would play and which they would not show up for.

In 1879, the *Cincinnati Gazette* proclaimed, "Baseball mania has run its course. It has no future as a professional endeavor."

Not for the last time, the story of the death of baseball was greatly exaggerated. Entrepreneurs saw the popularity of the game and kept trying to make it work as a business.

THE IMPACT OF COMPETITION

The National League eventually expelled Cincinnati from its ranks for selling beer in the stands and playing on Sundays, so the Reds started their own league called the American Association. The association added seven other members and began to sign players away from the National League. The two leagues were successful enough to coexist, eventually playing a postseason series between the respective league champions. By the mid-1880s, investors were making money on baseball, but the players were not.

Teams of the American League

In 1890, the players started yet another league, but three professional entities proved to be more than fans cared to support. Although the player's league lasted only one season, its existence had a crippling effect on the American Association, which lasted only one season after the player's league folded. The National League was the strongest, and as only the strong survive, it absorbed four association teams and expanded to 12.

LATE CENTURY TURMOIL

In small town America, baseball also was becoming more organized. Smaller professional teams were forming minor leagues, but even in these small towns, similar problems **persisted** gambling chief among them. In the National League, the problems spilled over onto the field. Players got into fistfights with umpires. Fans launched bottles and other projectiles from the stands at players and umpires, who would throw them right back at the fans. Owners had no control over their teams, and many had conflicts of interest as they had financial stakes in multiple teams. As players fought on the field, owners fought for control of the league.

Respectable patrons began to stay away as the games began to resemble riots rather than sport. Many again predicted the demise of professional baseball.

NEW CENTURY, NEW HOPE

Ban Johnson had a vision. Johnson was president of the four-team Western League, a minor league in the Midwest. He believed the game could be cleaned up, and with good people hired as players and umpires, baseball games could once again become desirable places for families to spend an afternoon. He aggressively began to pursue his plan in 1901.

With all the chaos in its ranks, the National League was forced to fold four teams, going down to eight. Having renamed the Western to be the American League, Johnson immediately moved into those four markets and declared the American League to be another Major League. He signed National League players by offering to double and in some cases triple their salaries.

In 1903, Johnson moved his Baltimore team to New York and renamed them the Yankees. For the next 50 years, the two eight-team leagues coexisted in peace with no significant changes. The first World Series was held that year as a best of nine between the Boston Americans of the American League and the Pittsburgh Pirates of the National League. Boston won in eight.

THE NATIONAL PASTIME

Many will say the first half of the 20th century was the golden age of baseball. Across the country, it became the outdoor pastime of choice, played in pastures and meadows in rural areas and on the paved city streets of urban America. The game was especially popular with the thousands of **immigrants** who arrived on America's shores in these years. Learning and playing the game helped their children fit in with their new friends. The game was its own language. For adult fans, from Polish to German to Italian, a home run spoke for itself in any tongue.

On the professional level, the game thrived. Owners could not build new concrete-and-steel stadiums fast enough. By its second year in 1905 (it was not played in 1904), the World Series was the biggest sporting event in the country.

Stability was, of course, a key component in the game's success and growth, but the biggest factor in the explosion of the game's popularity and the need to fill stadiums to watch it was the players, some of whom became the biggest stars in the country.

Text-Dependent Questions:

1. What is the name of the first professional baseball team?

2. In 1879, what newspaper proclaimed, "Baseball mania has run its course. It has no future as a professional endeavor"?

3. Who renamed the Western League to be the American League in 1901 and declared it to be another Major League?

Research Project:

As baseball is the U.S. national pastime, what other sports can you relate this phenomenon to in other countries? Who are the biggest stars around the world in other sports, and how does their fame and compensation for play compare to those of baseball players in the United States?

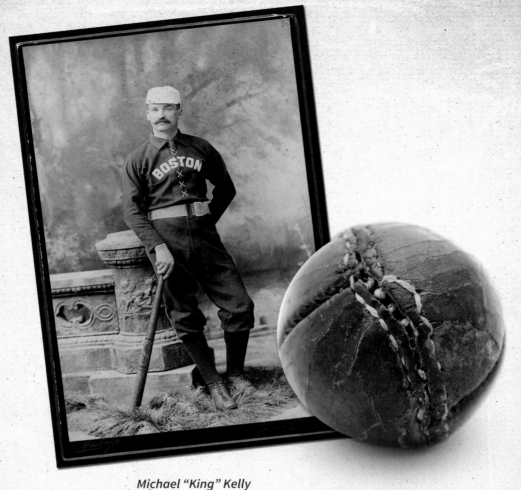

Michael "King" Kelly

Words to Understand:

flamboyant: having a very noticeable quality that attracts a lot of attention

shutouts: preventing of the opposite side from scoring

mangling: spoiling or ruining

CHAPTER

SLUGGERS AND SLINGERS

Decades before the advent of widely available mass media, the stories of heroic baseball exploits were just that, stories told from one to another. Fourth-hand eyewitness accounts and tales of what your uncle's barber's cousin read in his hometown paper spread the legends of baseball's early stars.

19TH-CENTURY STARS

Such was the lore of Michael "King" Kelly, a catcher for Chicago and Boston in the 1880s. Kelly is largely forgotten today, but in his time, his **flamboyant** style and outgoing personality made him a star off the field just as much as on it. Fans wrote songs about his antics.

Kelly was also a good player, leading the league in batting twice. But he was a notorious cheater. At the time, only a single umpire ran games. Legend has it that Kelly often would run directly from first base to third, or from second base directly home, skipping bases when the umpire was occupied with watching the ball.

"Wee" Willie Keeler was a right fielder who stood just 5'4" but swung the bat with authority. He hit .341 in his career from 1892 to 1910 with four New York City-based teams and the Baltimore Orioles. That average is the 14th best of all time. Keeler is also famous for his batting strategy, "Hit 'em where they ain't." He was a two-time batting champion.

DEAD-BALL DYNAMOS

Turn-of-the-century baseball was very different from today's game. The rules are all the same, but this was a time known as the "dead-ball era," where run scoring and home runs, in particular, were at the lowest point in baseball history. In 1908, for example, games averaged a total of 3.4 runs scored, the lowest average ever. It was a time dominated by pitchers.

One of the most dominant was Christy Mathewson of the New York Giants. Mathewso made his Big League debut in 1900. In the 1901 season, he won his first eight starts with four **shutouts**, and he quickly became a household name in New York and across the country. He led the Giants to the 1905 World Series, where he pitched three shutouts in six days. New York won the series against Philadelphia in five games. Mathewson's 373 career wins are still a National League record. Along with being one of the great pitchers of his time, Mathewson was also calm, dignified, and well-liked by his teammates.

The same could not be said for Detroit Tiger star Tyrus "Ty" Cobb. Cobb played outfield from 1905 to 1928 and did so with a mean streak and a nasty edge. This attitude led to Cobb being one of the most hated players in history, booed by fans and shunned by teammates. Cobb was unfazed, however, and used his attitude to make himself one of the game's premier players.

Crowds came to see the Tigers play just so they could boo Cobb. His reputation as a nasty player was forged on the base paths, where he would plow through, bowl over, or dig the spikes on his cleats into whoever got in his way. In the batter's box, however, is where Cobb shined. He was a .367 career hitter, still the Major League record, and he won more batting titles than anyone in history. Cobb collected more than 4,000 hits and stole nearly 900 bases, both feats that were not surpassed for 50 years. He was surly, mean-spirited, and ultracompetitive, all of which combined to fuel his anger toward the only personality in the sport more dominant than him—Babe Ruth.

THE BABE

George Herman "Babe" Ruth came along at the perfect time for baseball. In 1920, the Black Sox gambling scandal had broken, revealing that eight members of the Chicago White Sox took bribes to throw the 1919 World Series. It was an ugly stain that threatened to revive baseball's reputation of corruption, which so recently had been overcome. The owners named federal judge Kenesaw Mountain Landis to the post of commissioner of baseball, and he banned the eight players from the game for life. That was a necessary start. Ruth did the rest.

At the time, Ruth was one of the game's best pitchers. The left-hander helped Boston win the World Series in 1916 and 1918. Red Sox manager Ed Barrow noticed, however, that Ruth was also an outstanding hitter and began playing him in the outfield occasionally during the 1918 season when he wasn't pitching. He didn't remain a pitcher much longer.

Ruth displayed almost superhuman power at the plate. This was the dead-ball era, and power hitting was almost nonexistent. Ruth led the league in home runs in 1918 (with only 11) while splitting time as a pitcher. The National League leader hit only eight. Then, astoundingly, Ruth hit 29 home runs in 1919. The National League leader hit just 12. The rest of his Red Sox teammates combined to hit four. Much to Cobb's chagrin, Ruth was the talk of the game.

In the next year came what is probably the most discussed transaction in the history of sports. Red Sox owner Harry Frazee was in serious debt, so he agreed to sell Ruth's contract to the rival New York Yankees, despite Barrow's protests. The Yankees paid Boston $100,000, the highest ever for a player at the time. This transaction is said to have triggered the Curse of the Bambino. The Red Sox did not win another World Series for 86 years.

For the Yankees, however, the effect of the transaction was completely opposite to that on the Red Sox. Ruth hit an Earth-shattering 54 home runs for New York in 1920, not just more than any other player but also more than any other American League team. Ruthian became an adjective to describe towering home runs. His unprecedented feats drove the Black Sox scandal off of newspaper front pages. In 1921, he hit 59 more while batting .378. By the time he broke his own record by hitting 60 home runs in 1927, he was one of the most famous, and popular, people in the world. The dead-ball era was officially over.

Ruth led the Yankees to four World Series titles between 1923 and 1932, along the way winning the MVP in 1923 and the batting title in 1924 and leading the league in home runs 12 times. He retired in 1935 as the highest-paid player and drove up salaries for those who followed him. He made power hitting an in-demand commodity, changing the game forever.

Babe Ruth

THE BIG TRAIN

One of Ruth's rivals on the pitching mound before he became a full-time slugger was Walter "Big Train" Johnson of the Washington Senators. Johnson pitched from 1907 to 1927, winning 417 games. He was a dominant dead-ball pitcher, recording a 1.14 earned run average (ERA) in 1913, the sixth lowest of all-time. He led the league in strikeouts eight years in a row. He also led the league in wins six times and in ERA five times, including once in the live-ball era.

LIVE-BALL LEADERS

With the demise of the dead ball in 1920 (new technology was introduced that year that wound the balls tighter, and the spitball was outlawed), offensive numbers jumped. Ruth was in a class by himself (the next closest to his 54 homers in 1920 was 19), but scoring was on the rise.

Rogers Hornsby, second baseman for the St. Louis Cardinals, was the superstar of the era from the right side of the plate. Playing from 1915 to 1937, he took full advantage of the live ball. A .309 hitter in his first five years, Hornsby hit .397 from 1920 to 1925, leading the National League in hitting each of those years.

Ruth's closest competitor in the long-ball game was Jimmie Foxx, an infielder for Philadelphia and Boston. He played from 1925 to 1942, overlapping the last 11 years of Ruth's career. In that time, he twice beat Ruth to lead the league in home runs, including hitting 58 in 1932. In the 12 seasons from 1929 to 1941, he hit at least 30 homers each year.

Rogers Hornsby

DIZZYING FEATS

Ruth may have been the biggest personality in the game, but in the 1930s, a pitcher out of Arkansas came along. A favorite with the fans and the press, Jerome (Jay) Dean fully embraced the entertainment side of his profession. Dean gained the nickname Dizzy for his clubhouse antics and his **mangling** of the English language. Dizzy Dean played for the St. Louis Cardinals and liked to make bold predictions about how well he would do. One of his favorite sayings went like this: "It ain't braggin' if ya can back it up."

And back it up he could. Dean led the league in strikeouts his first two full seasons. In his third season in 1934, Dean hit his peak. He and his Cardinal teammates were known as the Gashouse Gang, and Dean was their leader. He won 30 games, the last time any National League pitcher has done that. *Time* magazine put him on the cover as he led the league in strikeouts again and won the MVP en route to leading the Cardinals to a World Series victory.

THE MANAGERS

In this heyday of baseball, the game's managers were often just as famous as the players.

John McGraw of the New York Giants was particularly popular with his home fans as he ran the Giants' dugout from 1902 to 1932. A great player for Baltimore before becoming a manager, McGraw was a man's man whom the players could relate to. Cantankerous and belligerent, he terrorized umpires, earning him 132 career ejections. He also led the Giants to 10 pennants and three World Series wins.

His opposite number in temperament was the dignified and always well-dressed Connie Mack. Mack managed the Philadelphia Athletics from 1901 to 1950. Mack's 50-year tenure is the longest ever in professional sports. When he finally retired at 87 years old, he had won nine pennants and five World Series.

Perhaps the most famous manager of the era was Casey Stengel. A notorious prankster, Stengel ran a loose clubhouse and had a fun-loving reputation with fans and writers. His managerial career started in Brooklyn in 1935, but he is most well-known for leading the New York Yankees to 10 pennants between 1949 and 1960. Those Yankees won the World Series seven times.

Connie Mack

Casey Stengel

John McGraw

Text-Dependent Questions:

1. What does legend say about Michael "King" Kelly?

2. What was the "dead-ball era"?

3. Who changed the game forever with this power hitting and retired in 1935 as the highest-paid player, driving up salaries for those who followed him?

 Research Project:

Not many players will ever enjoy the recognition of Babe Ruth. Take a closer look at his life. Write a report about his childhood, upbringing, training, and so on. Share your thoughts on how all of this shaped his career and opportunity in the sport.

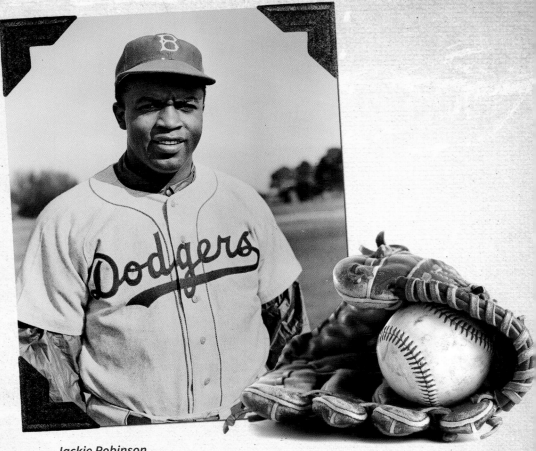

Jackie Robinson

Words to Understand:

segregated: restricted to one group, for example, on the basis of racial or ethnic membersh

integration: the act of combining into an integral whole, for example, integrating a racial, religious, or ethnic group

turnstiles: four horizontally revolving arms pivoting atop a post and set in a gateway or opening in a fence to allow the controlled passage of people

CHAPTER

A GAME FOR EVERYONE

The next significant era in baseball history is the one that changed the game most profoundly. In 1942, America found itself embedded in World War II. The whole country was affected as factories from coast to coast were converted to make weapons around the clock, and rolling blackouts went into effect.

Baseball was affected as well as hundreds of players were drafted into the service. President Roosevelt requested that baseball not shut down, however, as he said it was important to the country's morale.

With the war's end in 1945, the economy boomed, and Americans returned to what they loved—baseball. They did so in record numbers– 2.6 million fans turned out to watch the Indians in Cleveland that season, a record at the time. Thirteen of the 16 teams set attendance records in the five years following the war. Rosters swelled with the return of players from overseas. Fifty-nine minor leagues were in operation in the late 1940s.

Ted Williams and Johnny Sain in military uniform in the Fenway Park dugout during a Red Sox-Yankees game.

BASEBALL'S MOST SIGNIFICANT ROOKIE

Branch Rickey of the Brooklyn Dodgers is the godfather of the modern-day farm system, where minor league teams affiliate with Major League teams to develop young players. Rickey had 29 teams in operation after the war. But the minor league feeder system was not Rickey's only forward-looking endeavor.

In 1946, Rickey signed Jackie Robinson to play for his farm team based in Montreal. Robinson was the first black player to play in a white league since the leagues were **segregated** in the late 1800s. Black players since had been relegated to playing in a separate organized system dubbed the Negro Leagues.

Great players like Josh Gibson, John "Pop" Lloyd, Walter "Buck" Leonard, James "Cool Papa" Bell, and Leroy "Satchel" Paige never got the chance to show what they could have done in the Big Leagues in the prime of their careers. Paige famously debuted as a 42-year-old rookie with Cleveland in 1948 and pitched five seasons (mostly as a reliever) with the Indians and Browns, making two all-star teams. He was the first Negro League player to make the Hall of Fame.

The death of staunch segregationist Commissioner Kenesaw Mountain Landis in 1944 made the idea of integrating baseball a possibility. A year after signing Robinson to the minors, Rickey promoted him to the Dodgers for the start of the 1947 season. Enough cannot be said about the bravery Robinson exhibited, enduring threats, epithets, and continual harassment off the field and bean balls and spikings on the field. Robinson endured, however, and a few months later, Cleveland signed Larry Doby to integrate the American League.

INTEGRATION TAKES HOLD

The pace of **integration** was very slow at first. It took until 1959 until every team had at least one black player on the roster. But participation by black players steadily increased through the 1960s and 1970s. By 1981, nearly 19 percent of all players were black, a much higher percentage than exists in baseball today.

Latin players also benefitted from integration. There were a handful of Latin players in the Major Leagues when Robinson debuted, but that number increased steadily after 1947 as well. In 1951, Chico Carrasquel and Minnie Minoso became the first Latin all-stars. Latinos now make up about a quarter of all Major League players.

THE GAME CONTINUES TO CHANGE

In 1939, Rickey's Brooklyn Dodgers were the first team to televise one of its games. Announcer Red Barber and a single camera handled the broadcast duties that day. By 1949, all Major League teams broadcast at least a handful of their games on television.

With television rights and a constant stream of fans coming through the **turnstiles**, the owners were doing well. The players, however, did not feel that success was being fairly shared. As established, player rights belonged to the team that signed them forever, unless they were traded or sold to another team.

In 1969, three-time all-star and two-time World Series champion Curt Flood, an outfielder for St. Louis, sued the league when the Cardinals traded him to the woeful Philadelphia Phillies. He wanted the right to sign where he wanted if his current team did not want him. The case went in front of the Supreme Court in 1972. Flood lost, but two years before the decision, the league adopted a rule allowing players with at least 10 years of service, the last five with the same team, to veto any trade. Free agency for players came in 1975. Today, baseball is the highest-paying of all four major American professional sports.

On the field, the American League added the designated hitter, a player who did not play a field position but was allowed to bat in the pitcher's place without removing the pitcher from the game. The National League rejected the idea, and the two leagues operate the same way today.

Walter Lanier "Red" Barber

The Major Leagues experienced their first changes in 50 years in 1953 when the Boston Braves moved to Milwaukee. Over the next several years, many teams moved, most famously when both the Giants and the Dodgers left New York for California. The leagues expanded to add teams in the vacated cities. In 1961, the Angels and the original Washington Senators were added. By the end of the century, there were 30 Major League teams in all with the addition of teams in Arizona and the Tampa Bay area in 1998.

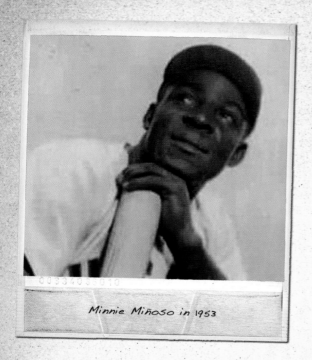

Minnie Miñoso in 1953

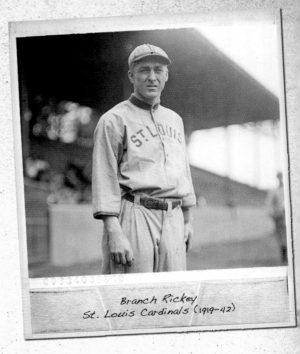

Branch Rickey
St. Louis Cardinals (1919-42)

The game also has expanded postseason participation over the years, going from two teams to four in 1969 and then from four to eight in 1994, including three division winners plus a wild card team in each league. In 2012, MLB added another wild card team in each league, and the two wild card teams play each other for the right to advance to their respective league's divisional series.

In the 21st century, staggering and historical change occurred in 2004, at least for Boston Red Sox fans. The Red Sox finally overcame the Curse of the Bambino that season. Not only did the Sox win the World Series by sweeping St. Louis, but they also got there by overcoming a 3-0 deficit to their bitter rivals, the New York Yankees. They are the only team in baseball history to come back from a 3-0 postseason deficit.

Perhaps the biggest change to the games played before and after World War II is the fact that night baseball grew from a novelty to the norm. But on the field, the novelties were few. Babe Ruth would find batting helmets and gloves strange, and his outfielder's mitt unusually large, but standing in the batter's box staring out at a pitcher, he would be right at home.

Ruth's modern-day counterparts might have a more difficult time adjusting to a dead ball or tiny gloves, but in today's game, baseball's superstars are a dominant bunch, and the fans flock to see them play.

Text-Dependent Questions:

1. Who was the first black player to play in a white league since the leagues were segregated in the late 1800s?

2. In 1939, which team was the first to televise one of its games?

3. What is the highest-paying of all four major American professional sports?

Research Project:

Research Jackie Robinson. Learn more about his role in desegregating the sport of baseball. Use his story as inspiration to support someone or a group that still faces discrimination today.

Clayton Kershaw

Words to Understand:

unanimously: characterized by or showing complete agreement

lucrative: profitable, moneymaking, remunerative

defected: having deserted a cause or country, especially to adopt another

44

CHAPTER

MODERN-DAY STARS

Fans love the long ball. Offensive firepower gets a lot of attention in baseball. Managers, on the other hand, love the three-hit shutout. They, along with savvy baseball fans, appreciate the impact of a dominant starting pitcher.

THE HURLERS

In the 2010s, no pitcher was more dominant than the Los Angeles Dodgers' Clayton Kershaw. From 2011 to 2014, Kershaw led the Major Leagues in ERA. In that breakout 2011 season, Kershaw was in his fourth year with L.A. after debuting as the youngest player in baseball in 2008.

In 2011, Kershaw won 21 games and led the league in strikeouts, which combined with his league low ERA made him the pitching Triple Crown winner at just 23 years old. The left-hander also won his first Cy Young award (and a Gold Glove for good measure). Kershaw finished either first or second in Cy Young voting for four straight years. When he won his third award in 2014, Kershaw also was voted MVP of the entire league. He was the first pitcher to win the National League MVP in 46 years. Kershaw threw his first career no-hitter that season against Colorado (striking out 15 Rockies) on his way to a 21-3 record and a 1.77 ERA.

Kershaw's American League counterpart was Detroit's Justin Verlander. Verlander also won the pitching Triple Crown in 2011, leading all of baseball with 24 wins and 250 strikeouts with a 2.40 ERA. The Tiger's right-hander also threw his second career no-hitter that season against Toronto and went on to **unanimously** win the Cy Young award. Like Kershaw in 2014, Verlander was voted league MVP for 2011.

Verlander was voted American League Rookie of the Year in 2006 and was voted to the American League All-Star Team in five straight seasons, from 2009 to 2013. In that 2009 season, he led the league in wins and strikeouts but finished third in the Cy Young voting. In 2012, he was the runner-up in the Cy Young voting after going 17-8 while leading the league in strikeouts and finishing second in ERA. Verlander's success was no surprise to baseball experts. After a stellar college career at Old Dominion University in his native state of Virginia, the Tigers drafted him second overall in the 2004 draft.

As much as Verlander's success was expected, few players in baseball history have had greatness predicted to the degree that it was for Stephen Strasburg. The right-hander was drafted first overall in 2009 by the Washington Nationals. After his sophomore and junior seasons at San Diego State, he left Washington little choice. He went 21-4 with an ERA under 1.5 and more than 300 strikeouts. After being drafted, he set the record for the most **lucrative** contract for an initial signing at $15.1 million.

Stephen Strasburg

Strasburg recorded 14 strikeouts to win his Nationals debut in 2010 but blew out his elbow 12 starts into the season, missing the rest of the year and most of the next. In 2012, his innings were limited as part of the recovery from his injury, so despite leading Washington to the playoffs, he never pitched in the postseason. Strasburg had an off year in 2013 but rebounded to lead the league in strikeouts in 2014.

Like Strasburg, Venezuelan Felix Hernandez has long borne the weight of high expectations. By the time he was 14, he could already throw 90 mph (145 kph). This drew the attention of a Seattle Mariners scout who recommended that they pay attention to the flame-throwing right-hander. Seattle signed him at just 16 years old.

He debuted with the Mariners in August of 2005 at age 19. By 2009, he had hit his stride in the Majors. He was named to the All-Star Team, led the league with 19 wins, and had a 2.49 ERA and 217 strikeouts. He finished second in the Cy Young voting. In 2010, he won the Cy Young. His record was just 13-12, but he led the league with a 2.27 ERA and nearly 250 innings pitched. Fernandez was voted to the All-Star Team in each of the next five seasons, from 2011 to 2015. In 2014, he again led the league in ERA at 2.14. Nicknamed King Felix, he held dominion over American League hitters for more than a decade.

THE FIREMEN

If starters are the kings of the pitching staff, then closers are the crown princes. Craig Kimbrel is next in line to the throne. Kimbrel broke in with the Atlanta Braves in 2010 and became the full-time closer to start the next season. The right-hander had a glorious rookie season in 2011. He was named to the National League All-Star Team and broke the record for saves by a rookie in a season, collecting 46, a total that led the National League. He also set a Major League record for most consecutive scoreless innings pitched with 38 1/3. Kimbrel was unanimously chosen as the National League Rookie of the Year.

Kimbrel proceeded to lead the league in saves in each of the next three seasons, tying the record for consecutive league-leading seasons. In 2014, he recorded his 400th strikeout, getting to that milestone faster than any player in history. The Braves traded their all-time saves leader to San Diego in 2015.

Aroldis Chapman is next in the line of succession. The Cuban left-hander took the route to the Major Leagues that was necessary by players from his country. He **defected** from the Cuban national team during a tournament in Holland. He fled to Andorra and then petitioned Major League baseball for free agency.

The Cincinnati Reds were the winning bidders for Chapman's services, and he became their full-time closer in 2012. That season, Chapman was a revelation, striking out batters at a furious clip. He had 122 strikeouts in 71 2/3 innings in that all-star season, the first of four straight trips to the All-Star Game, all with more than 30 saves. In 2014, he struck out more than 52 percent of the batters he faced, the highest rate in baseball history. The reason he is so hard to hit is his fastball, which was clocked at more than 105 mph (169 kph), the fastest speed ever recorded.

Aroldis Chapman

Greg Holland is a completely different type of pitcher than Chapman. Chapman is 6'4" (1.9 m) and 215 lbs. (97.5 kg) and fires missiles. Holland stands just 5'10" (1.8 m) and under 200 lbs. (90.7 kg). Yet Holland is every bit as effective.

Holland came up with the Kansas City Royals in 2011, going 5-1 with a 1.80 ERA. The next season, he became the full-time closer in July. In 2013, Holland rose to the top of the league. He converted 47 of 50 save chances, breaking the team record of 45 saves in a season set by Hall of Famer Dan Quisenberry. Holland was named to the All-Star Team and ended the year with a minuscule 1.21 ERA. The 2014 season was a near carbon copy, with 46 saves, a 1.44 ERA, and another All-Star Game appearance. Kansas City went to the World Series that year, and Holland tied records for saves in a series (4) and in the playoffs (7). He was voted best reliever in the American League in 2014.

The World Series provided the stage for Francisco Rodriguez to burst into the spotlight. In 2002, the rookie right-hander had never won a Major League game, but he won a spot on the Anaheim Angels roster in the postseason as a September call-up. He mesmerized hitters from the Yankees, the Minnesota Twins, and the San Francisco Giants with his wicked curveball on the way to winning the series. He racked up five postseason wins along the way, becoming the youngest pitcher ever to win a World Series game.

Rodriguez followed up his amazing first experience in the Majors with a stellar career, including six All-Star Game appearances. He led the league in saves three times, including setting the Major League record for saves in a season with 62 in 2008. In 2013, he recorded his 300th career save as a member of the Milwaukee Brewers. He is one of the top 10 pitchers in saves in Major League history.

Giancarlo Stanton

Mike Trout

THE SLUGGERS

It is a long-standing Major League tradition that the power hitters play the outfield. Seven of the top 10 home run hitters of all time patrolled the outfield for the majority of their careers. To be considered among the best, players need to have multiple tools at their disposal, but if one of those tools is the three-run homer, that goes a long way.

Giancarlo Stanton was taken in the second round of the 2007 draft by the Florida Marlins. Shortly after his Major League debut in 2010, he hit his first home run with the bases loaded. That grand slam was an early indicator of things to come for Stanton.

In 2011, Stanton topped 30 home runs for the first time in his career with 34. The next season, he improved yet again, this time hitting 37 with 86 runs batted in (RBI) and leading the league in slugging. Stanton's power earned him a trip to the All-Star Game. He also hit .290, his best batting average to date. He missed two months of the 2013 season with an injury but rebounded in 2014 with another all-star season. Stanton hit 37 home runs with 105 RBI, leading the league in both homers and slugging. That was all the Marlins needed to see. In December 2014, they signed their right fielder to a $325 million contract, the richest in sports history. Stanton made his third All-Star Team in 2015.

Unlike Stanton, Mike Trout is much more than just a power hitter. The Los Angeles Angels' center fielder broke into the Majors as a 19-year-old call-up in 2011. In 2012, his first full season was one for the ages. Not only did he hit 30 home runs, but he also led the Major Leagues in stolen bases and runs scored. He also routinely made highlight reel catches in center field and was the unanimous Rookie of the Year. He was also the runner-up for MVP, losing only because Miguel Cabrera was the first Triple Crown winner in 45 years.

Trout was the runner-up for MVP the next season as well, once again leading the league in runs scored. In 2014, Trout's third consecutive all-star season, he led the league in runs and RBI and this time won the MVP with a unanimous vote. His combination of speed, power, .305 batting average, and great catches made him the most versatile player in baseball.

As Trout was finishing in the top two in the American League MVP voting from 2012 to 2014, Andrew McCutchen was matching him stride for stride in the National League. The Pittsburgh Pirates center fielder finished top three in MVP voting in his league in each of these three seasons. McCutchen won the award in 2013, hitting .317 with 21 home runs, 28 steals, and 84 RBI. He also made the All-Star Team five straight years from 2011 to 2015.

Miguel Cabrera

A five-tool player like Trout, McCutchen has stolen at least 20 bases five times and uses that speed to track down balls in centerfield. He was the National League Gold Glove winner at the position in 2012. He led Pittsburgh to the postseason from 2013 to 2015, the first playoff appearances for the Pirates since 1992. His impact on a franchise that had lost 100 games as recently as 2010 cannot be overstated.

Jose Bautista primarily makes an impact on baseballs, and he does so frequently and with ferocity. The right fielder from the Dominican Republic was not taken until the Pirates picked him in the 20th round in the 2000 draft. He broke into the Big Leagues with Pittsburgh in 2006 but did not find his stroke until after he was traded to the Toronto Blue Jays in 2008.

Bautista struggled at the plate until the 2010 season, when he earned his nickname, "Joey Bats." That's when he permanently moved from part-time third baseman to full-time outfielder and began showing results from his work with a new hitting coach. This was the first of five straight all-star seasons for Bautista, who led the Majors in home runs with 54. He hit 43 to lead baseball again the following season and finished in the top four in MVP voting both seasons. A sub-.260 career hitter, Bautista is feared mostly for his power.

Bryce Harper will be one of the most feared hitters in the National League for the next 15 years. The Washington Nationals outfielder was the 2012 Rookie of the Year at 19 years old, but he was not just the best rookie. His season was good enough to earn an invitation to the All-Star Game. Harper's 254 total bases and 57 extra-base hits were the most ever for a player under age 20. He was an All-Star in 2013 and again in 2015, when he produced an NL leading 42 home runs and 118 runs scored to win the MVP. It is exactly what Washington expected when they selected Harper with the first pick of the 2010 draft.

THE GLOVE MEN

Miguel Cabrera is feared for all aspects of hitting. Often referred to as the best hitter of his generation, the Venezuelan-born Cabrera came from humble beginnings. Undrafted, he signed with the Florida Marlins in 2003. He was called up for just 86 games that season, but it culminated in a postseason appearance for the Marlins, where Cabrera hit .265 with 4 home runs and 12 RBI to help Florida win the World Series. He hit .313 in his five seasons with Florida, where he was voted to four All-Star Teams.

In 2008, Florida traded their all-star third baseman to Detroit, where his remarkable career continued. Cabrera has driven in at least 100 runs in every full season, twice leading the Majors in RBI. He led the league in home runs twice, hitting at least 30 nine times. He led the league in hitting three straight years, from 2011 to 2013. He was MVP in 2012, where he won the Triple Crown for the first time since 1967. He was MVP in 2013 as well, the first back-to-back winner in 20 years.

When Cabrera looked across to the second base position during each of his all-star appearances from 2010 to 2014, he saw Robinson Canó. Canó spent the first nine seasons of his career anchoring the infield for the New York Yankees in stellar fashion. Along with the consecutive all-star appearances, he also finished in the top six in the MVP voting in each of those seasons.

Canó was signed right out of high school in the Dominican Republic in 2001. He joined the Yankees in 2005, immediately cracking the lineup of a team that was perennially in the postseason. The Yankees were in the playoffs in seven of Canó's nine seasons there, the highlight of which was a World Series win in 2009. A .309 hitter with five 20+ home run seasons with the Yankees, Canó was also a slick fielder, winning two Gold Gloves. He signed with Seattle as a free agent for the 2014 season.

As he lay on the field in May 2011 with a shattered leg and shredded ankle, getting to the 2014 season must have seemed like a lofty goal for Gerald "Buster" Posey. The San Francisco Giants' catcher had just been run over at home plate in a game against Florida. The result of the collision was season-ending surgery to repair three torn ligaments and a broken fibula, and there was concern for the future career of the 2010 Rookie of the Year. Posey was coming off a rookie season where he backstopped the Giants to a World Series championship. Without Posey, the Giants missed the 2011 playoffs.

To say Posey recovered nicely would be an understatement. In 2012, he had an all-star and MVP season, belting 24 home runs with 103 RBI while leading the league in hitting at .336. The Giants returned to the playoffs and won the World Series again. After another all-star season in 2013, Posey led the 2014 Giants back to the World Series and another championship.

When Posey's injury forced him to miss most of the 2011 season, the door opened for another team to win the National League pennant, and Albert Pujols made sure his St. Louis Cardinals were that team. The Cardinals' first baseman hit .299 with 37 home runs and 99 RBI to lead his team to the playoffs. He hit .353 in the postseason en route to a World Series win against Texas. It was the second World Series win in Pujol's sure-fire Hall of Fame career.

Albert Pujols

The Dominican-born Pujols became a ten-time all-star and three-time MVP after breaking into the league as Rookie of the Year in 2001. He did not win MVP in what may have been his best season, 2003. That year he led the Majors in hitting at .359 with 43 home runs and 124 RBI. He hit more than 40 home runs six times, leading the league twice. He is in the top 20 all-time for career home runs.

Pujols is one of the best players ever to lace up a pair of cleats. But is he one of the truly greatest ever? In the long history of baseball, there are many candidates to that title.

Text-Dependent Questions:

1. After being drafted, which player set the record for the most lucrative contract for an initial signing at $15.1 million?

2. In 2012, his first full season in the majors, which player not only hit 30 home runs but also led the Major Leagues in stolen bases and runs scored?

3. Which Venezuelan-born player is often referred to as the best hitter of his generation?

Research Project:

The Society for American Baseball Research has a Baseball Biography Project where anyone can submit comprehensive biographical articles on people who played or managed in the major leagues. Write about your favorite star of today or yesterday and submit your article to the project to see if you get published! More information can be found at http://sabr.org/bioproject.

HONUS WAGNER

STAN MUSIAL

HOYT WILHELM

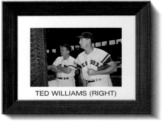

MARIANO RIVERA

BABE RUTH

TREVOR HOFFMAN

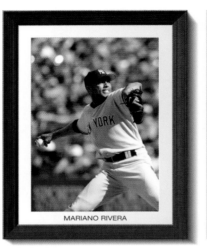

TED WILLIAMS (RIGHT)

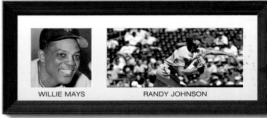

WILLIE MAYS   RANDY JOHNSON

DENTON "CY" YOUNG

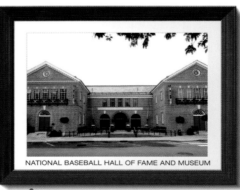

NATIONAL BASEBALL HALL OF FAME AND MUSEUM

CHRISTY MATHEWSON (RIGHT)

The National Baseball Hall of Fame and Museum is located in Cooperstown, New York. It was dedicated in 1939 as a place to honor the game. The first five members selected in 1936 were Ty Cobb, Babe Ruth, Honus Wagner, Christy Mathewson, and Walter Johnson. Twenty more players were selected before the inaugural induction ceremony in 1939. The Baseball Writers Association of America currently selects players to be inducted. Players must be named on at least 75 percent of ballots to be inducted. Players are removed from the ballot after 20 years but may be considered by the Veteran's Committee. About 300,000 people visit the Hall of Fame annually.

CHAPTER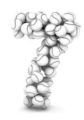

BASEBALL'S GREATEST PLAYERS

More than any other sport, to those who love and follow it, statistics are the language of baseball. That language has developed new dialects in recent years, with the rise of Sabermetrics, the new-school statistics touted most prominently by people such as baseball historian and statistician Bill James. While stats like value over replacement player (VORP) and on-base plus slugging (OPS) have become more prevalent in the discussion of how to measure greatness in the sport since the 1990s, they have not yet outstripped the traditional batting average and RBI in the lexicon of the casual fan.

Sabermetric statistics may well be baseball's language of the future, but fans love the language of the past—home runs, RBI, ERA—these are the building blocks of the traditional language.

The language of statistics has inspired the most passionate discussion that exists among baseball fans: who is the best of all time? That discussion gets tricky when comparing players across baseball's eras, but breaking down the statistics to make that comparison is a large part of the fun.

If statistics are the language of baseball, then the record book is its bible. In no sport are statistical records more hallowed than baseball. The conversation about the greatest players is tied inextricably to the record book.

For this reason, the so-called steroid era in baseball was so damaging and is so reviled. From 1994 to 2007, home run numbers jumped sharply. From 1965 to 1994, the 50-home-run plateau was reached only twice. From 1995 to 2007, it happened 23 times. This has been attributed to the use of performance-enhancing drugs like anabolic steroids and growth hormones.

Players who broke some of baseball's most sacred records in this time have been linked to or admitted using these banned substances. Therefore, players like Barry Bonds, Mark McGwire, Sammy Sosa, Alex Rodriguez, and Roger Clemens are not being considered in this discussion of the greatest players. Like Pete Rose before them, the all-time hits leader who is banned for life for gambling, these players damaged the integrity of the game and will have a very difficult, if not impossible, time getting into the Hall of Fame.

This discussion is reserved for those who played the game within the rules and excelled at it on their own merits.

STARTERS

The ace of the staff, the stopper, the go-to guy—a team's number one starter is all of these things, counted on to win when his turn in the rotation arrives. Few did it better than Cy Young.

Denton "Cy" Young pitched for Cleveland from 1890 to 1898. He went on to pitch for four other teams in both leagues through the 1911 season. Young pitched more innings, completed more games, and both won and lost more games than any pitcher in history. He was the game one starting pitcher for Boston in the first World Series. The current award for best pitcher of the season is named for him.

Along with Young, Christy Mathewson was the other dominant pitcher of the dead-ball era. Only in the final three seasons of his 17-year career did his ERA climb over 3.00. He pitched all but one game of his career with the New York Giants, for whom Mathewson led the National League in wins four times. He led the league in ERA five times, including a career-best 1.14 in 1909. Mathewson won the pitching Triple Crown twice and the World Series twice. No National League pitcher in history has more career wins.

Walter Johnson racked up career wins and strikeouts at an alarming rate from 1907 to 1927. The Washington Senators star was the era's preeminent power pitcher. Johnson led the league in strikeouts a Major League record 12 times, twice recording more than 300 in a season. His 3,509 career strikeouts stood as a record for 56 years. He was more than just a flamethrower, however. He also led the league in wins six times and in ERA five times, claiming pitching's Triple Crown three times in the process.

Greg Maddux never was considered to be a power pitcher in his Hall of Fame career from 1986 to 2008. He only weighed 170 lbs. (77.1 kg), and yet he is exactly one position behind Walter Johnson on the career strikeout leaders list, which puts him in the top 10 all-time. Maddux's talent was his control. He is the only pitcher in history with more than 300 wins, more than 3,000 strikeouts, and fewer than 1,000 walks.

Maddux won the National League Cy Young award four straight times with Chicago and then Atlanta, which had never been done before. He led the league in wins three times and ERA four times and is considered to be the best fielding pitcher of all time. Maddux won 18 Gold Gloves in his career, a record for any position.

The only other pitcher besides Maddux to win four straight Cy Young awards is Randy Johnson. He accomplished the feat with the Arizona Diamondbacks from 1999 to 2002. He also won the award with Seattle in 1995. At 6'10" (2.1 m) and 225 lbs. (102.1 kg), Johnson is one of the most overpowering pitchers ever to take the mound. Known as "The Big Unit," Johnson mowed down hitters with abandon, leading the league in strikeouts nine times.

But strikeouts don't win Cy Youngs. Johnson also led the league in ERA four times, including 2002, when he won the Triple Crown with 24 wins, 334 strikeouts, and a 2.32 ERA. The power was his signature, however. Johnson struck out more than 300 hitters six times and is second all-time in career whiffs.

Which pitcher is the best? It would be fascinating to witness a pitching matchup between Maddux and Mathewson circa 1960. Mathewson might be the slight favorite to get the win.

Denton "Cy" Young

Randy Johnson

Christy Mathewson

RELIEVERS

When the game is on the line, and the starter is out of gas, the relief pitcher suddenly becomes the most important player on the field. Specialty pitching is a relatively new phenomenon in baseball but is now a career aspiration for pitchers rather than a last resort.

Hoyt Wilhelm pitched for nine teams in his 21-year career from 1952 to 1972. He appeared in 1,070 games, all but 52 of those in relief. Behind his vaunted knuckleball, the right-hander racked up 124 wins, which is an MLB record for relievers. He was a five-time all-star, including for the 1959 season, when he led the league with a 2.19 ERA. His New York Giants went to the World Series in 1954, where Wilhelm recorded one save in 2 1/3 perfect innings in the Giants' four-game sweep of Cleveland.

When Wilhelm retired in 1972, Rollie Fingers was just hitting his stride as a reliever for the Oakland Athletics. The right-hander pitched for Oakland from 1968 to 1976. His first of seven all-star seasons was 1973, including four straight from 1973 to 1976. The A's also won three straight World Series from 1972 to 1974. Fingers was World Series MVP in 1974.

Trevor Hoffman   *Hoyt Wilhelm*   *Mariano Rivera*

Fingers is famous for his signature handlebar mustache and for pioneering the role of the late-inning closer. He led the league in saves three times, including in 1981, when he won both the Cy Young and the American League MVP, the first reliever to win both awards in the same season.

Dennis Eckersley is the last reliever to win both the Cy Young and MVP in the same season. That year was 1992, the last of his six all-star seasons. The lanky right-hander began his career as a starting pitcher with Cleveland, but his Hall of Fame-worthy years came when he joined Oakland as a reliever in 1987. Eckersley led the league with 45 saves in 1988. He made the All-Star Team as a reliever that season and in three of the next four, including 1992. He also won a World Series in 1989.

The year after Eckersley won the MVP as a reliever, Trevor Hoffman debuted as a rookie right-handed relief pitcher for Florida. Halfway through the 1993 season, the Marlins traded Hoffman to San Diego, where he became a seven-time all-star. Hoffman averaged more than 40 saves a season after becoming a full-time closer in 1994. In 1998, he had 53 saves to lead the league, and then eight years later he had 46 saves to do the same. In both of those seasons, he was the runner-up in the Cy Young voting. He retired in 2010 with 601 saves, the second most all-time.

The only reliever with more saves than Hoffman is Mariano Rivera. His career was staggering. The right-handed Panamanian went to 13 All-Star Games in 19 seasons and played on five World Series championship teams with the New York Yankees. In 1999, Rivera was named World Series MVP in a four-game sweep of Atlanta. The career Yankee led the American League in saves three times. He saved more than 40 games nine times.

By traditional or new-school statistics, Rivera is head and shoulders above his rivals for the title of the best. He leads in wins above replacement (WAR), win probability added (WPA), walk rate, and strikeout rate. Some quibble with the fact that most of Rivera's saves were of the one-inning variety. Rivera, however, has a career ERA as a reliever of 2.06, lowest of any reliever with at least 200 innings. It wasn't all about the saves, of which he had the most ever. He retired with a record 652 and is the best reliever ever to play the game.

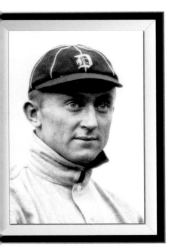

Ty Cobb

Babe Ruth

Ted Williams

OUTFIELDERS

Ty Cobb was not a popular man in his time. By all accounts, he was a violent racist off the field. On the field, however, there is no denying he was a great ballplayer.

Cobb won 12 batting titles and led the league in steals six times and in RBI four times. He won the Triple Crown in 1909 when he hit .377 with nine home runs and 107 RBI. In 1911, he was league MVP when he hit .420 and drove in 127 runs, both career highs. When Cobb retired in 1928 after 24 seasons, his career batting average was .366, still an MLB record.

If Babe Ruth did not spend the first five years of his career as a pitcher, his famous hitting exploits would be all that more impressive. Considering that he hit 29 home runs during a season in the dead-ball era, he is widely considered to be the best power hitter ever. His 714 career home runs stood as the record for nearly 40 years.

Ruth led the league in home runs 12 times, hitting 50 or more four times. He was MVP in 1923 and won the Triple Crown in 1924. The Yankee slugger is the most famous hitter in baseball history.

Ted Williams was known as the Splendid Splinter. The splinter part was about his lean frame. The splendid part was about his mean bat. The Boston Red Sox legend played 19 seasons. He led the league in hitting six times, including in 1941, when he hit .406. No player has hit .400 or better since.

Williams won Triple Crowns in 1942 and 1947. In his first season back from the military after a three-year absence, he was voted MVP in 1946. In 1949, he had a career-high 43 home runs and 156 RBI to earn a second MVP. Williams's career .344 batting average is the seventh best ever.

Willie Mays could do it all on the baseball diamond. The quintessential five-tool player, he could hit for power and average, run, catch, throw, and field. He led the league in hitting in 1954, one of two MVP seasons. He led the league in home runs four times. He led the league in steals four times and won a dozen consecutive Gold Gloves in center field.

Mays went from Rookie of the Year in 1951 for the Giants to retiring in 1973 with 660 home runs, which is top five all-time. He could do it all, and very few did any of it better.

The year after Mays retired, Hank Aaron broke the biggest record in American sports, Babe Ruth's career home run record of 714. His 755 career home runs are second only to the tainted total of Barry Bonds. Much like Mays, however, Aaron was more than just a power hitter. He led the league in hitting twice and is a career .305 hitter. In 1957, he led the league with 44 home runs and 142 RBI to win the MVP.

Aaron also stole 20 or more bases six times, won three Gold Gloves, and has more RBI than anyone who ever played. Hammerin' Hank always will be remembered, however, for the home run he hit on that April day in 1974.

The players in the outfield category are some of the true legends of the game. Ruth's legend casts the biggest shadow, but in terms of baseball greatness on the field, Mays stands tallest of all.

| Rogers Hornsby | Jimmie Foxx | Lou Gehrig |

INFIELDERS

Baseball is America's pastime, and once upon a time, collecting baseball cards was the passion of 10-year-old boys across the country. Trading cards are almost as old as the sport. As far back as 1909, companies produced cards with player likenesses. Shortstop Honus Wagner, a nonsmoker, was on a series of cards produced by a tobacco company. When he demanded they cease, a limited number had already been released to the public. In good condition, that card today is worth more than $2 million.

Wagner was one of the best players in baseball at the time. He hit .338 in his first Big League season with Louisville in 1897. He joined the Pittsburgh Pirates in 1900 and went on to lead the league in batting eight times and in stolen bases five times in his 21-year Hall of Fame career.

Rogers Hornsby took over from Wagner as the best middle infielder in the game when he arrived in St. Louis for his first full season as the Cardinal shortstop in 1916. Hornsby hit .313 that season and went on to lead the league in hitting seven times.

Hornsby won the Triple Crown in 1922 and 1925. In 1922, he became the first player to hit .400 and 40 home runs. In that 1925 season, his 39 home runs, 143 RBI, and .403 average earned him the MVP award. Hornsby earned a second MVP in 1929 after joining the Chicago Cubs.

Hornsby was the highest-paid player in the game when Lou Gehrig debuted as a New York Yankee rookie in 1923. A native New Yorker, Gehrig quickly became a local hero. He became the regular first baseman in 1925 and didn't miss a game for the rest of his career, earning him the nickname the Iron Horse.

In 1927, Gehrig won his first MVP, hitting .373 with 47 home runs and a then-record 173 RBI. He finished in the top five in MVP voting eight times, including a second win in 1936. He is a career .340 hitter, the 16th best all-time.

Jimmie Foxx, like all players in the 1920s and 1930s, played in the shadow of Gehrig, Ruth, and the mighty Yankees. But the spotlight of history shows he was every bit their peer.

Foxx played first base for 20 seasons, mostly with Philadelphia and Boston. He won his first batting title in 1932 with the A's. He won two more, in 1933 and 1938. In both of those seasons, he was named American League MVP and won the Triple Crown in 1933. He led the league in RBI in all three of those seasons. He hit more than 500 career home runs and drove in more than 100 runs from 1929 to 1941.

Stan Musial's rookie season in 1941 was with the St. Louis Cardinals. He played first base or left field from 1941 to 1963. A seven-time batting champion with a .331 career average, Musial got a lot of hits. His total of 3,630 is fourth best in history.

Musial never hit 40 home runs in a season but hit more than 20 for 10 years in a row. He also drove in more than 100 runs on 10 occasions. He had a record 24 all-star appearances and won three MVPs. In 2010, the 90-year-old Musial was awarded the Presidential Medal of Freedom, the highest civilian award of the United States.

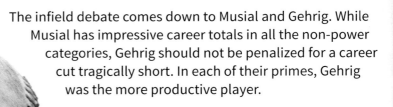

The infield debate comes down to Musial and Gehrig. While Musial has impressive career totals in all the non-power categories, Gehrig should not be penalized for a career cut tragically short. In each of their primes, Gehrig was the more productive player.

Career Snapshots

Starters

#51 RANDY JOHNSON 1988–2009

303-166 record
3.29 ERA
4,875 K

#31 GREG MADDUX 1986–2008

355-227 record
3.16 ERA
3,371 K

WALTER JOHNSON 1907–27

417-279 record
2.17 ERA
3,509 K

CHRISTY MATHEWSON 1900–16

373-188 record
2.13 ERA
2,507 K

CY YOUNG 1890–1911

511-316 record
2.63 ERA
2,803 K

Relievers

#42 MARIANO RIVERA 1995–2013

82-60 record
2.21 ERA
652 Saves

#51 TREVOR HOFFMAN 1993–2010

61-75 record
2.87 ERA
601 Saves

#43 DENNIS ECKERSLEY 1975–98

197-171 record
3.50 ERA
390 Saves

#34 ROLLIE FINGERS 1968–85

114-118 record
2.90 ERA
341 Saves

#31 HOYT WILHELM 1952–71

143-122 record
2.52 ERA
228 Saves

*All the above athletes are members of the Hall of Fame
*No player numbers used until 1930

Outfielders

#44 HANK AARON 1954–76

.305 avg.
755 HR
2,297 RBI

#24 WILLIE MAYS 1951–73

.302 avg.
660 HR
1,903 RBI

#9 TED WILLIAMS 1939–60

.344 avg.
521 HR
1,839 RBI

#3 BABE RUTH 1914–35

.342 avg.
714 HR
2,214 RBI

TY COBB 1905–28

.366 avg.
117 HR
1,933 RBI

Infielders

#6 STAN MUSIAL 1941–63

.331 avg.
475 HR
1,951 RBI

#3 JIMMIE FOXX 1925–45

.325 avg.
534 HR
1,922 RBI

#4 LOU GEHRIG 1923–39

.340 avg.
493 HR
1,995 RBI

#4 ROGERS HORNSBY 1915–37

.358 avg.
301 HR
1,584 RBI

HONUS WAGNER 1897–1917

.328 avg.
101 HR
1,732 RBI

Words to Understand:

prominence: the state of being important, well-known, or noticeable

demographic: a group of people defined by a characteristic, such as age, race, or region

glacial: very slow

CHAPTER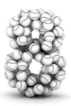

THE FUTURE OF BASEBALL

Looking ahead into the crystal ball of the sport, it is difficult to predict sweeping changes given how relatively few have occurred in the game to this point. But perhaps the rate of change will be one of the changes down the road for America's pastime.

A GOLDEN ERA

Baseball may not have the **prominence** it once did on the American sports scene, but the future health of the game is not in doubt. It is entrenched in the fiber of the country. In fact, Commissioner Bud Selig declared in 2013, "We're in a golden era. We are in numbers that nobody could have dreamed possible." Attendance figures bear out Selig's assertion. The 10 highest-drawing seasons in baseball history have all occurred between 2004 and 2014. More than 73 million fans now attend ballparks every summer.

Given the many reports in the early part of the century that baseball was floundering, especially in comparison to the NFL, proclamations of prosperity may seem surprising. Losing the 1994 World Series due to the longest strike in baseball history left a sour taste in the mouths of fans. The steroid use that was rampant in the game in the years immediately after also left many fans disillusioned.

THE GAME RECOVERS

Those dark days, however, have been quickly forgotten. By 2015, there had been 20 years of labor peace, revenue sharing was in place that truly helped small market clubs, and a regional television strategy was filling team coffers. Total revenue was more than $7.5 billion, up more than 500 percent from 1995.

There are indications as well that baseball is succeeding in reaching a younger generation of fans, one of the things the game had struggled to do that had many predicting its collapse. One of those is the embrace of social media, as MLB has made itself more accessible in the digital space, engaging young fans in the arenas they frequent.

DIGITAL REVOLUTION

All sports, including baseball, compete with all other forms of entertainment. Baseball's brand of entertainment has been trending toward being popular with an ever-aging **demographic**. But the game is working toward attracting a younger fan base. Besides social media engagement efforts, teams like the Boston Red Sox and Los Angeles Dodgers are creating content geared specifically toward that fan who is always on, always connected. It is true digital content, not just digital ads trying to push traditional platforms. MLB now has an Advanced Media division, and with other teams catching on, baseball's future is trending digital.

The digital reach of the game also is expanding to TV audiences. Baseball is working on enhancing its broadcast product with a digital component, engaging viewers on that second screen studies show they are typically using while watching TV. Real-time stats and custom replays are just some of the possibilities.

THE BEST GETS BETTER

Baseball prides itself on having the best in-stadium experience. That's where the casual fan turns up. The die-hard will always watch on TV, but that less passionate fan will go to the game for the live experience. Future ballparks are being designed to make that experience even better.

The Atlanta Braves' new ballpark north of the city is one example. It will have the highest percentage of seats situated near the playing surface. Fans will enter on the outfield side, where the entrance includes a pedestrian mall with shops and restaurants that are open to the public every day. The stadium also will have air-conditioned concourses to keep fans cool between innings during those scorching Georgia summers.

SPEED UP AND GET IT RIGHT

One of the primary reasons the in-stadium experience is so important in baseball is that the on field experience unfolds less quickly than it does in other sports. Detractors of the sport will say it is downright slow. Games often take more than three hours to complete. The people who run the game are aware that this pacing is perceived as **glacial** and are working to improve it in the future. Rules designed to speed up the timing between pitches and between batters have been enacted, and the league will review their impact to continue adjusting them in the future.

Baseball has been the slowest of the major sports to embrace video technology. The future trend looks to be toward expanding replay use, however. Modifications are being considered that will allow managers to challenge plays until they have a challenge that is not successful, and replay use will be expanded in the postseason as well.

INTERNATIONAL APPEAL

Baseball may be America's pastime, but several other countries have embraced the game. It is famously popular in Japan, home to the best professional league outside of the United States. Japan has produced superstars from Hideo Nomo to Ichiro Suzuki, players who have excelled not just in their home leagues but in the Majors as well.

Fans of Major League baseball also will be very familiar with the popularity of the game in Latin America. More than a quarter of MLB's players in 2015 were of Latin descent, and that percentage is expected to grow into the future.

The World Baseball Classic embodies the international appeal of the sport. This international tournament is held every four years. It involves 16 teams in a double elimination format, which evolves to single elimination after the first round. Teams from 18 countries had qualified to play in the first three installments of the event, which began in 2006, and that number is likely to expand along with the game's global appeal.

Yankee Stadium, New York Yankees

Wrigley Field, Chicago Cubs

Fenway Park, Boston Red Sox

Miller Park, Milwaukee Brewers

FUTURE STARS

Pitcher José Fernández is a prime example of the influence the sport has had outside America's borders. The Cuban-born Fernández was National League Rookie of the Year for the Miami Marlins in 2013. In a spectacular season when he was second in the league with a 2.19 ERA and sixth in strikeouts, the rookie finished third in the Cy Young award voting. His strikeout rate of 9.81 per nine innings led the league, and he was in the top 10 all-time for pitchers under 21 in several advanced statistical categories. The right-hander will dominate hitters for years to come.

Fernández's Cuban countryman, José Abreu, will be one of the more difficult hitters to dominate in baseball for the next 10 years. The Chicago White Sox first baseman was the 2014 Rookie of the Year in the American League, but he was not just the best rookie. His season was good enough to earn Abreu an invitation to the All-Star Game. He hit .317 with 36 home runs and 107 RBI while leading the league in slugging. In 2015, he hit 30 home runs and drove in more than 100 again (101). Chicago's gamble to give the untested Abreu a $68 million contract when he defected from Cuba in 2013 looks like it will pay off in a big way.

THE PASTIME LIVES ON

Baseball's stars will continue to lure fans to the ballpark well into this century, a place filled with the same sights, sounds, and smells enjoyed by the generations of last century. Through labor strife and steroid scandals, the game endures. The crack of the bat, the cheer of the crowd, the runner sliding safely into home—these are the moments that build the memories that ensure baseball always will be a part of summer in America.

José Fernández

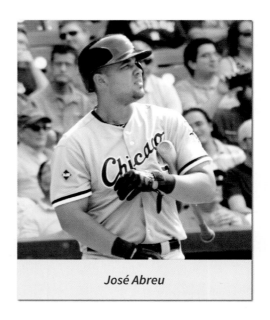

José Abreu

Text-Dependent Questions:

1. How many million fans now attend ballparks every summer?

2. Give some examples of how future ballparks are being designed to make the in-stadium experience even better.

3. Which country is home to the best professional league outside of the United States?

Research Project:

Visit a baseball stadium and feel the experience and excitement of being at a game. Take notes on what you think are the most important aspects of that experience. Give suggestions on ways to increase attendance or enhance the overall experience.

GLOSSARY OF BASEBALL TERMS

all-star: a player chosen by fans and managers to play on the All-Star Team against the opposing league in the MLB All-Star Game in the middle of the season. The league that wins hosts the first game of the World Series.

backstop: a screen behind home plate that keeps wild pitches or foul balls from going into the stands; also another name for the catcher.

balk: when the pitcher pretends to pitch to try to catch a runner off base. When the umpire calls a balk, all base runners advance to the next base.

box: the rectangle where the batter stands, also called the batter's box, or the area where the pitcher fields the ball.

breaking ball: any pitch that curves in the air: a curve ball, slider, screwball, sinker, or forkball.

bunt: a ball batted for a short distance to help the batter to reach first base or to advance another runner on base, while the defense makes the out at first.

change-up: a slow pitch that throws off a batter's timing.

cleanup: the fourth hitter in the lineup, usually the best hitter on the team. If all three runners get on base before the cleanup hitter, it's up to him to get them home, likely with a home run.

closer: the pitcher called in during the last innings to preserve a lead.

curve: a pitch that spins the ball with a snap of the wrist, forcing it to curve near the plate.

designated hitter (DH): the player who hits for the pitcher. This position was created in 1973 and is used only in the American League.

doubleheader: when two teams play twice on the same day, one game after the other.

double play: two outs in one play, for example, a strikeout and a base runner being thrown out or when two runners are called out on the bases.

error: a defensive mistake resulting in a batter reaching base or getting extra bases. The official scorer calls errors.

fastball: a pitch thrown at high speed, usually more than 90 miles per hour (145 km/h) in MLB.

foul ball: when a ball is hit into foul territory. A hitter's first two fouls count as strikes, but a batter can't be called out on a foul ball.

grand slam: a home run when runners are on all the bases.

ground-rule double: when a ball is hit fairly but then goes out of play (for example, over the home run fence after it bounces) but because of an agreed-upon rule for the ball park, the player gets to second base.

grounder: when the batter hits a ball that bounces in the infield.

hit-and-run: a play in which a base runner runs right when the pitcher pitches, and the hitter tries to hit the ball into play to help the runner get two bases or avoid a double play.

home run: when a batter either hits a fair ball out of the field of play or when the batter runs around all the bases to score before he or she is thrown or tagged out.

inning: one of nine periods in a regular game. Each inning gives each team a turn to hit until they make three outs. If the game is tied after nine innings, the game goes into extra innings until one team is ahead by at least one run at the end of an inning.

knuckleball: a pitch with as little spin as possible that moves slowly and unpredictably. The pitcher grips the ball with his fingertips or knuckles when throwing the pitch.

line drive: when a batter hits the ball hard and low into the field of play, sometimes called "a rope."

mound: where the pitcher pitches from. It is a packed dome of dirt, 60 feet, 6 inches (18.4 m) from the back of home plate and no more than 10 inches (25.4 cm) high. The pitcher uses a rectangular slab of rubber at its center to push himself toward the plate when pitching.

no-hitter: a game in which one team gets no base hits.

pick-off: when a pitcher or catcher throws a runner out, catching him or her standing off the base.

pinch-hit: when a hitter bats for another player. The player who does not bat leaves the game.

relief pitcher: a pitcher who comes into the game to replace another pitcher.

sacrifice: when a batter makes an out on purpose to advance a runner (for example, a sacrifice bunt or fly ball). A sacrifice play is not an official at bat for the hitter.

slider: a pitch that is almost as fast as a fastball but curves. The pitcher tries to confuse the batter, who may have trouble deciding what kind of pitch is coming.

stolen base: when a base runner runs right when the pitcher pitches, and if the pitch is not hit, makes it to the next base before being thrown out.

strikeout: when a batter gets a third strike, either by missing the ball or not swinging on a pitch that is in the strike zone.

triple play: three outs in one play. This is very rare.

walk: when the pitcher throws four pitches outside the strike zone (called balls by the umpire) but before throwing three strikes, allowing the hitter to walk to first base.

Oriole Park at Camden Yards

CHRONOLOGY

1858 Amateur players organize the National Association to schedule games and standardize rules.

1869 The Cincinnati Red Stockings field the first all-professional team.

1876 William A. Hulbert organizes the National League.

1901 Ban Johnson creates the American League.

1903 The first modern World Series is played, with the Boston Red Sox defeating the Pittsburgh Pirates.

1920 Federal Judge Kenesaw Mountain Landis is named baseball's first commissioner.

1935 The first night game is played in the Major Leagues in Cincinnati.

1938 The first baseball game is televised, Cincinnati at Brooklyn.

1939 The National Baseball Hall of Fame opens in Cooperstown, New York.

1947 Jackie Robinson debuts with the Dodgers.

1954 Three franchises relocate to Kansas City, Milwaukee, and Baltimore, the first change in 50 years.

1958 The Dodgers and Giants move to California.

1961 Roger Maris breaks Babe Ruth's single-season home run record.

1966 The MLB Players Association is formed.

1968 The strike zone is reduced and the pitching mound is lowered to 10 inches (25.4 cm).

1973 The American League adopts the designated hitter rule.

1974 Hank Aaron breaks Babe Ruth's career home runs record.

1977 The American League expands to 14 teams.

1993 The National League expands to 14 teams.

1994 The World Series is cancelled due to a player's strike.

1998 MLB expands to 30 total teams.

2008 Baseball implements an instant replay review system.

Baseball Today: In 2016, Ken Griffey Jr. was elected to the MLB Hall of Fame with the highest percentage of votes in history (437 of 440 for 99.32%). On the same ballot, steroid-era star Mark McGwire received just 12.3% of the vote, falling shy of the needed 75% for the 10th straight year, meaning he is no longer eligible for election despite his 583 career home runs.

FURTHER READING:

Sports Illustrated. *Sports Illustrated Baseball's Greatest: 2013.* New York: Sports Illustrated, ILL edition 2013.

Lyons, Douglas B. *100 Years of Who's Who in Baseball: 2015*. Guilford, CT: Lyons Press, 2015.

Dobrow, Larry. *Derek Jeter's Ultimate Baseball Guide 2015.* New York: Jeter Publishing, 2015.

Herman, Gail. *Who Is Derek Jeter?* New York: Grosset & Dunlap, 2015.

INTERNET RESOURCES:

Baseball Hall of Fame http://baseballhall.org/

ESPN http://espn.go.com/

Baseball Reference http://www.baseball-reference.com/

Major League Baseball http://mlb.mlb.com/home

VIDEO CREDITS:

Baseball Hall of Fame: (pg 4, 54, 78) https://www.youtube.com/watch?v=zCfFe5_kqig

Ruth Calls His Shot: (pg 8) http://m.mlb.com/video/topic/6479266/v3218817/bb-moments-42-ws-gm-3-babe-ruths-called-shot

Gehrig's Farewell Speech: (pg 9) https://www.youtube.com/watch?v=ZN2k76DHkgk

Jackie Robinson Integrates Baseball: (pg 10) http://m.mlb.com/video/v2527060/bb-moments-41547-jackie-robinson-breaks-barriers/?mlbtax=bb_moments

The Shot Heard 'Round The World: (pg 11) http://m.mlb.com/video/topic/6479266/v3218951/bb-moments-10351-the-giants-win-the-pennant

Willie Mays' Catch: (pg 12) http://m.mlb.com/video/v3218956/bb-moments-54-ws-gm-1-willie-mays-amazing-catch/?mlbtax=bb_moments

Mazeroski's Home Run: (pg 13) http://m.mlb.com/video/topic/6479266/v3218957/bb-moments-60-ws-gm-7-bill-mazeroskis-walkoff

Aaron Passes Ruth: (pg 14) http://m.mlb.com/video/v4429231/4874-aaron-hits-hr-no-715-to-pass-babe-ruth

Fisk Waves it Fair: (pg 15) http://m.mlb.com/video/topic/6479266/v3224115/bb-moments-75-ws-gm-6-carlton-fisk-waves-it-fair

Gibson's Limp-Off Homer: (pg 16) http://m.mlb.com/video/v3364800/bb-moments-88-ws-gm-1-hobbled-gibsons-pinch-hr

Ripken Passes Gehrig: (pg 17) http://m.mlb.com/video/v3251272/bb-moments-9695-cal-ripken-mlbs-new-iron-man/?mlbtax=bb_moments

Jeter Flips It Home: (pg 18) http://m.mlb.com/video/v3134880/nyyoak-gm-3-jeter-cuts-down-runner-with-iconic-flip

The Curse Is Broken: (pg 19) http://m.redsox.mlb.com/bos/video/v19983103/ws2004-gm4-red-sox-complete-a-fourgame-series-sweep/?query=red%2Bsox%2Bcurse

QR CODES AND LINKS TO THIRD-PARTY CONTENT

You may gain access to certain third-party content ("Third-Party Sites") by scanning and using the QR Codes that appear in this publication (the "QR Codes"). We do not operate or control in any respect any information, products, or services on such Third-Party Sites linked to by us via the QR Codes included in this publication and we assume no responsibility for any materials you may access using the QR Codes. Your use of the QR Codes may be subject to terms, limitations, or restrictions set forth in the applicable terms of use or otherwise established by the owners of the Third-Party Sites. Our linking to such Third-Party Sites via the QR Codes does not imply an endorsement or sponsorship of such Third-Party Sites, or the information, products or services offered on or through the Third-Party Sites, nor does it imply an endorsement or sponsorship of this publication by the owners of such Third-Party Sites.

PICTURE CREDITS

INDEX

In this index, page numbers in ***bold italics*** font indicate photos or videos.

INDEX